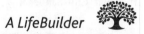 *A LifeBuilder*

C000275417

PLEASING GOD

9 studies
for individuals or groups

Jack Kuhatschek

With Notes for Leaders

Scripture Union is an international Christian charity working with churches in more than 130 countries.

Thank you for purchasing this book. Any profits from this book support SU in England and Wales to bring the good news of Jesus Christ to children, young people and families and to enable them to meet God through the Bible and prayer.

Find out more about our work and how you can get involved at:

www.scriptureunion.org.uk (England and Wales)
www.suscotland.org.uk (Scotland)
www.suni.co.uk (Northern Ireland)
www.scriptureunion.org (USA)
www.su.org.au (Australia)

ISBN 978 1 78506 259 9

First published in the United States by InterVarsity Press.
© Jack Kuhatschek

First published in the United Kingdom © Scripture Union 2010; this edition 2015, 2016.

Scripture quotations, unless otherwise indicated, are taken from the Holy Bible, New International Version. Copyright © 1973, 1978, 1984 by International Bible Society. Anglicisation copyright © 1979, 1984, 1989. Used by permission of Hodder and Stoughton Limited.

British Library Cataloguing-in-Publication data: a catalogue record for this book is available from the British Library.

Printed in India by Thomson Press India Ltd

Image credit: carlosalvarez/iStock by Getty Images

Contents

GETTING THE MOST OUT OF *PLEASING GOD* ———— 5

1 **Perfectly Pleasing**   Hebrews 10:1-25———— 9

2 **Amazed by Grace**   John 8:1-11 ———— 13

3 **Offering Yourself to God** Romans 12:1–8———— 17

4 **Living by Faith**   Hebrews 11:1-16———— 21

5 **Looking at Your Heart**   1 Samuel 16:1-13 ———— 25

6 **Pursuing Moral Purity**   1 Thessalonians 4:1-12 —— 28

7 **Keeping the Peace**   Romans 14 ———— 32

8 **Obeying His Commands**   1 John 3:11-24 ———— 36

9 **Keeping Your Balance**   Psalm 73 ———— 40

Leader's Notes———— 44

Getting the Most Out of *Pleasing God*

In the year 1162 King Henry II had a brilliant plan to curb the growing power of the church. He nominated his close friend and chancellor, Thomas Becket, to become archbishop of Canterbury. In one decisive move Henry would thereby control both church and state.

But his plan backfired. When Becket was consecrated, a profound change came over him. He suddenly realized that he had a higher loyalty than serving the king. Now he wanted with all his heart to please God and to do his will. In the movie *Becket,* that moment of transformation is captured in one of the archbishop's prayers. As he kneels before the Lord, Becket says,

> Please, Lord, teach me now how to serve you with all my heart, to know at last what it really is to love, to adore, so that I may worthily administer your kingdom here upon earth, and find my true honor in observing your divine will. Please, Lord, make me worthy.

If you are a Christian, then like Becket you have a deep desire within your heart to please God. The apostle Paul writes in 2 Corinthians 5:9-10, "We make it our goal to please him, whether we are at home in the body or away from it. For we must all appear before the judgment seat of Christ, that each one may receive what is due to him for the things done in the body, whether good or bad."

Like children performing for our parents in a backyard play, we long to receive the applause, the approval, the divine "well done" from our heavenly Father. In an essay entitled "The Weight of Glory," C. S. Lewis writes,

The promise of glory is the promise, almost incredible and only possible by the work of Christ, that some of us, that any of us who really chooses, shall actually survive that examination, shall find approval, shall please God. To please God . . . to be a real ingredient in the divine happiness . . . to be loved by God, not merely pitied, but delighted in as an artist delights in his work or a father a son—it seems impossible, a weight or burden of glory which our thoughts can hardly sustain. But so it is. (*The Weight of Glory and Other Addresses* [New York: Macmillan, 1949], p. 13.)

In these Bible studies we will explore what it means to please God. We will discover why faith in Christ is the foundation of such a life, trust and commitment its ongoing expression, and godly character its result. We will also look at why pleasing God is not a matter of legalistic rules and regulations but rather flows from a clear conscience and a sincere heart.

As you begin this study, I pray with the apostle Paul "that you may live a life worthy of the Lord and may please him in every way: bearing fruit in every good work, growing in the knowledge of God" (Col 1:10).

Suggestions for Individual Study

1. As you begin each study, pray that God will speak to you through his Word.

2. Read the introduction to the study and respond to the personal reflection question or exercise. This is designed to help you focus on God and on the theme of the study.

3. Each study deals with a particular passage—so that you can delve into the author's meaning in that context. Read and reread the passage to be studied. If you are studying a book, it will be helpful to read through the entire book prior to the first study. The questions are written using the language of the New International Version, so you may wish to use that version of the Bible. The New Revised Standard Version is also recommended.

4. This is an inductive Bible study, designed to help you discover for yourself what Scripture is saying. The study includes three types of questions. *Observation* questions ask about the basic facts: who, what when, where and how. *Interpretation* questions delve into the meaning of the passage. *Application* questions help you discover the implications of the text for growing in Christ. These three keys unlock the treasures of Scripture.

Write your answers to the questions in the spaces provided or in a personal journal. Writing can bring clarity and deeper understanding of yourself and of God's Word.

5. It might be good to have a Bible dictionary handy. Use it to look up any unfamiliar words, names or places.

6. Use the prayer suggestion to guide you in thanking God for what you have learned and to pray about the applications that have come to mind.

7. You may want to go on to the suggestion under "Now or Later," or you may want to use that idea for your next study.

Suggestions for Members of a Group Study

1. Come to the study prepared. Follow the suggestions for individual study mentioned above. You will find that careful preparation will greatly enrich your time spent in group discussion.

2. Be willing to participate in the discussion. The leader of your group will not be lecturing. Instead, he or she will be encouraging the members of the group to discuss what they have learned. The leader will be asking the questions that are found in this guide.

3. Stick to the topic being discussed. Your answers should be based on the verses which are the focus of the discussion and not on outside authorities such as commentaries or speakers. These studies focus on a particular passage of Scripture. Only rarely should you refer to other portions of the Bible. This allows for everyone to participate in in-depth study on equal ground.

4. Be sensitive to the other members of the group. Listen attentively when they describe what they have learned. You may be surprised by their insights! Each question assumes a variety of answers. Many questions do not have "right" answers, particularly questions that aim at meaning or application. Instead the questions push us to explore the passage more thoroughly.

When possible, link what you say to the comments of others. Also, be affirming whenever you can. This will encourage some of the more hesitant members of the group to participate.

5. Be careful not to dominate the discussion. We are sometimes so eager to express our thoughts that we leave too little opportunity for others to respond. By all means participate! But allow others to also.

6. Expect God to teach you through the passage being discussed and through the other members of the group. Pray that you will have an enjoyable and profitable time together, but also that as a result of the study you will find ways that you can take action individually and/or as a group.

7. Remember that anything said in the group is considered confidential and should not be discussed outside the group unless specific permission is given to do so.

8. If you are the group leader, you will find additional suggestions at the back of the guide.

1

Perfectly Pleasing

Hebrews 10:1-25

In Greek mythology a man named Sisyphus, who was the founder and king of Corinth, was condemned by Zeus to push a heavy rock up a steep hill eternally. Every time Sisyphus would near the pinnacle of the hill, the stone would roll back to the bottom, where he would begin the laborious process one more time.

Surprisingly, many Christians feel that way about the weight of their sins. No matter how hard they try, no matter how many times they repent or resolve to do better, they believe they can never do enough. They can never satisfy God's demands, much less please him.

GROUP DISCUSSION. Why do you think so many Christians feel so unacceptable to God and so unable to please him?

PERSONAL REFLECTION. What sins are weighing on you as you begin this study? Take time now for confession.

In Hebrews 10:1-25 the author tells us to stop trying to do the impossible. Although we can never do enough to please God on our own, Jesus has made us perfectly pleasing—forever. *Read Hebrews 10:1-25.*

1. What are some of the contrasts you noticed as you read the passage?

2. According to verses 1-4, why was the Old Testament practice of offering animal sacrifices an endless exercise in futility (vv. 1–4)?

3. Why did these annual sacrifices make worshipers feel worse rather than better about their sins?

4. What are some of the pointless and ineffective ways people try to get rid of their guilt today?

5. How is God's pleasure in Christ contrasted with God's response to offering and sacrifices (vv. 5–10)?

6. If God was not truly pleased with the animal sacrifices of the Old Testament, then why do you think the law required them to be made (vv. 5, 8)?

7. What contrasts does the author of Hebrews make between the Old Testament priests and sacrifices versus the sacrifice of our great priest, Jesus Christ (vv. 11–18)?

8. If Christ's one sacrifice has not only brought us complete forgiveness but also "made us perfect forever," then why do you think we often feel just as guilty as worshipers in the Old Testament (note v. 2)?

9. In both the Old Testament tabernacle and temple, a thick curtain separated worshipers from the "Most Holy Place," where the presence of God dwelt. Why can we now enter God's presence with confidence rather than a guilty conscience (vv. 19–23)?

10. Because of what Christ has done for us, what four responses ("let us . . .") should we have toward God and each other (vv. 22–25)?

How is each of these responses vital for spiritual health and growth?

11. In which of these areas would you most like to grow?

Thank God for the fact that through Christ you have been forgiven, made perfect forever, and cleansed from a guilty conscience. Ask him to help you respond to his grace and forgiveness in the appropriate ways.

Now or Later

The author of Hebrews urges us to "draw near to God with a sincere heart in full assurance of faith." Plan a special time and place to draw near to God today or this week. Take your Bible with you and find a favorite spot—such as a nearby park or a quiet place in the library or a comfortable chair in your home—and spend time in God's presence, knowing that he accepts you completely in Christ.

2

Amazed by Grace

John 8:1-11

Victor Hugo's novel *Les Misérables* tells the story of a man named Jean Valjean, who served nineteen years of hard labor for the crime of stealing bread. When he was finally released, Valjean was a hardened, tough ex-convict.

But one day his life was transformed by forgiveness. A kind bishop invited him to stay in his home for the night. After the bishop and his sister were asleep, Valjean stole the family silver and ran off into the night. The next morning, he was captured by three policemen and brought back to the bishop.

"So here you are!" the bishop cried to Valjean. "I'm delighted to see you. Had you forgotten that I gave you the candlesticks as well? They're silver like the rest, and worth a good 200 francs. Did you forget to take them?"

After the policemen had gone, the bishop gave the candlesticks to Valjean, who was speechless and trembling. "Do not forget; do not ever forget," the bishop said, "that you have promised me to use the money to make yourself a new man."*

GROUP DISCUSSION. Why do you think the bishop's act of grace was a turning point in Valjean's life?

PERSONAL REFLECTION. Who has shown you grace? Reflect prayerfully. Thanking God for the actions that come to mind.

In John 8 we discover that a life which is pleasing to God does not begin with commitment or sheer determination. Like Valjean and the woman caught in adultery, we must be overwhelmed by grace. *Read John 8:1-11.*

1. How do you think you would feel if you were caught in the act of committing adultery, dragged before a large crowd and exposed for your sin (vv. 1-3)?

2. Roman law would not permit Jews to carry out executions. How did the woman's accusers hope to trap Jesus no matter how he responded (vv. 4-5)?

3. Since adultery by its very nature is done in private, this "trap" may have been premeditated and planned by the teachers of the law and the Pharisees. If this is true, what does it reveal about the character of the woman's accusers?

4. Why do you think Jesus pauses to write on the ground rather than answering the question immediately (v. 6)?

5. When Jesus finally straightens up and responds, how does he catch the accusers in their own trap (v. 7)?

6. Why should our own guilt make us reluctant to throw verbal stones at those who have sinned?

7. After being confronted by Jesus, why do you think the accusers left one at a time, beginning with the oldest (vv. 8-9)?

8. Finally, only Jesus and the woman are left facing each other (vv. 9-11). What similarities do you see between this part of the story and the bishop's words to Jean Valjean?

9. Even if you've never committed adultery, how is your encounter with Jesus similar to the woman's?

10. " 'Then neither do I condemn you,' Jesus declared. 'Go now and leave your life of sin' " (v. 11). How does this kind of grace provide you with a powerful motive for a changed life?

Ask God for the grace to "leave your life of sin," whatever those sins may be. Pray for the motivation to live a life that is pleasing to him.

Now or Later

If Jesus were to say to you, "Go and leave your life of sin," what two or three specific sins might come to your mind? Write these down on a piece of paper, but do not show the paper to anyone else. Now write the words, "Neither do I condemn you" in bold letters across the sins you have written. Then destroy the paper and resolve by God's grace to repent of these sins he has already forgiven.

*Quoted in Philip Yancey, *What's So Amazing About Grace?* (Grand Rapids, Mich.: Zondervan, 1997).

3

Offering Yourself to God

Romans 12:1-8

In his book *Lectures to My Students* the great British preacher Charles Spurgeon wrote that "it is our duty and our privilege to exhaust our lives for Jesus. We are not to be living specimens of men in fine preservation, but living *sacrifices,* whose lot is to be consumed; we are to spend and to be spent, not to lay ourselves up in lavender, and nurse our flesh."

GROUP DISCUSSION. Describe a time in your life when you gave yourself passionately and completely to a project or a cause.

PERSONAL REFLECTION. Spurgeon describes two types of people: those who are "living specimens" and those who are "living sacrifices." Which description best fits you and why?

Spurgeon's words were based on one of the most challenging passages in the New Testament: Romans 12:1–8. In these verses Paul urges us to offer ourselves fully and completely to God. *Read Romans 12:1–8.*

1. How would you describe the tone of this passage?

2. Paul bases his appeal on God's mercy (v. 1), which Paul described in the first eleven chapters of Romans. Why must we grasp what God has done for us before we do anything for him?

3. In the Old Testament, worshipers killed an animal and sacrificed it to God. How does that kind of sacrifice contrast with what Paul asks of us (v. 1)?

4. One person has said that the trouble with a "living sacrifice" (v. 1) is that it keeps crawling off the altar! In what ways do you find it challenging to live for Jesus?

5. J. B. Phillips translates verse 2 as, "Don't let the world around you squeeze you into its own mold." In what ways do you feel pressured to conform to worldly values and practices?

6. The word *transformed* (v. 2) comes from the same Greek word from which we get *metamorphosis*. How can renewing our minds help us to experience a spiritual metamorphosis?

7. People often think of sacrificial living as something unpleasant. Yet why do you think it ultimately pleases not only God (v. 1) but us also (v. 2)?

8. What guidelines does Paul give us for thinking about ourselves (v. 3)?

9. How can our physical bodies help us to understand the way each of us fits into the body of Christ, the church (vv. 5–6)?

10. Paul's list of spiritual gifts in verses 6–8 is not meant to be exhaustive (see "Now and Later" for other key passages). Based on your past experiences, what "gifts" do you think God has given you for serving others?

How can you offer these gifts not only to God but also to the church?

Thank God for the incredible mercy he has given you in Christ. As a worshipful response, offer yourself to God as a living sacrifice, asking him for the grace to serve him and others.

Now or Later

Read the other key passages on spiritual gifts: 1 Corinthians 12; Ephesians 4; 1 Peter 4. What do these verses reveal to you about the spiritual gifts God has given you?

4

Living by Faith

Hebrews 11:1-16

Hudson Taylor, the founder of the China Inland Mission, once faced a crisis in a hospital he supervised. An anxious worker came to him and said, "Mr. Taylor, we have run out of food. We are down to our last bag of rice." Instead of panicking, Taylor responded with typical faith: "Then God's provision must be very near!"

GROUP DISCUSSION. In "Pudd'nhead Wilson's New Calendar" Mark Twain wrote, "There are those who scoff at the school boy, calling him frivolous and shallow. Yet it was the school boy who said, 'Faith is believing what you know ain't so.'" How would you evaluate his definition?

PERSONAL REFLECTION. Think of a Christian you know who truly lives a life of faith. What impresses you about the way that faith is demonstrated?

Throughout history men and women have learned to trust God, to depend on him for their physical and spiritual needs. In Hebrews 11, the biblical Hall of Fame, we will meet some of those people and discover why their faith was so pleasing to God. *Read Hebrews 11:1-16.*

1. Notice that all of the people mentioned in this chapter are from the Old Testament. If you were to add one New Testament character (other than Jesus) to the biblical Hall of Fame, who would be at the top of your list and why?

2. How do you respond to the author's description of faith in verse 1?

3. Why does it take faith to believe that "the universe was formed at God's command" (v. 3)?

4. Abel is the first biblical example of faith (see Genesis 4:2-5 for more information). Why would offering his sacrifice "by faith" make it better and more commendable than Cain's (v. 4)?

5. The Genesis account of Enoch says nothing about his faith (see Genesis 5:18-24 for more information). Why then do you think the author of Hebrews views Enoch as an example of faith (v. 5)?

6. Why is faith absolutely essential if we want to please God (v. 6)?

7. How was building the ark an act of faith for Noah (v. 7; see Genesis 6—9 for more information)?

In what sense did Noah's faith condemn the world?

8. What parallels do you see between Noah's time and our own, and between Noah's response and ours?

9. In verses 8-12 the author of Hebrews mentions three examples of Abraham's faith. How would each of these situations have required faith?

10. Even though Abraham and the other people mentioned in this passage experienced God's faithfulness firsthand, the author makes a remarkable statement: "All these people . . . did not received the things promised" (v. 13). Why must God's promises ultimately await a future fulfillment (vv. 13-16)?

11. What unseen, unfulfilled realities give you hope and shape your daily life?

Ask God to enable you to please him more and more as you rely on his promises and live by faith.

Now or Later

God's Hall of Fame (or Hall of Faith) also includes many people from church history. Read a biography of either Hudson Taylor, George Muller, Amy Carmichael, D. L. Moody, Corrie ten Boom or some of the other giants of the faith from recent times. As you read, ask God to show you how you can follow their example of faith.

5

Looking at Your Heart

1 Samuel 16:1-13

In the book *Selling of the President,* author Joe McGinnis emphasized that in politics, image is everything. A candidate must exude confidence, charm and good looks. Never mind the real issues of the campaign. A broad smile, a warm handshake and the ability to look good on camera are much more important for selling the political product to the consumer—the registered voter.

GROUP DISCUSSION. How does a person's appearance affect your initial opinion of him or her?

PERSONAL REFLECTION. Have you unfairly judged someone by appearance lately? Take a few moments to confess anything that comes to mind.

Israel's first king, Saul, was the ideal candidate—tall, handsome and impressive. Unfortunately, he was also foolish and disobedient. As

Israel's second king is chosen, the Lord rejects worldly standards of leadership and chooses a man after his own heart. *Read 1 Samuel 16:1-13.*

---

1. In what ways does the mood of this passage—and the various characters in the passage—shift as the scene progresses?

---

2. What specific instructions does the Lord give Samuel for anointing a new king (vv. 1-3)?

---

3. Why did Samuel suppose that Eliab was the Lord's anointed (vv. 6-7; see 17:13)?

---

4. According to verse 7, how does God's perspective differ from ours?

---

5. The Lord tells Samuel that people look at "the outward appearance" (v. 7). What sorts of "outward" things do we tend to look at in people?

---

6. How does our culture reinforce our emphasis on appearance?

---

7. Why are outward qualities an unreliable way to judge a person?

8. If you had been given the job of finding the next king of Israel, why would David have been an unlikely choice?

In what sense was he also a good choice (see v. 18)?

9. Why do you think the Lord has Samuel look at each of Jesse's sons before revealing that he has chosen David (vv. 6-12)?

10. When the Lord looks at our hearts, what specific qualities do you think he values most, and why?

11. Our physical heart is strengthened through a healthy diet and regular exercise. What can we do to strengthen our heart spiritually?

Ask God to help you focus more on your heart than on your appearance. Pray that he will develop those qualities within you that please him.

Now or Later

Write down two or three ways you can begin to strengthen your heart spiritually. Then commit to starting a spiritual exercise program, where you can work on developing some of the qualities mentioned in question 10.

6

Pursuing Moral Purity

1 Thessalonians 4:1-12

In Homer's great epic *Odyssey* he tells of two mythical creatures called Sirens, who had the heads of women and the bodies of birds. The Sirens sang melodies so beautiful that passing sailors were lured to their deaths on the rocky shoreline. In order to protect himself and his crew from this danger, King Odysseus ordered his men to plug their ears with beeswax and to tie him to the mast.

GROUP DISCUSSION. Sexual temptation has wrecked the lives of countless people in every generation. Why do you think sexual tempation is so great in our society?

PERSONAL REFLECTION. In what ways are we exposed to sexual temptation through television, movies, magazines and other media?

In 1 Thessalonians 4:1-12 Paul warns us about the tempting allure of sexual immorality. If we are to please God, we must take the proper precautions. *Read 1 Thessalonians 4:1-12.*

---

1. What major topics does Paul focus on in verses 1-12?

---

2. According to Paul the Thessalonians were already pleasing God by the way they lived. Why then do you think Paul urges them to "do this more and more" (v. 1)?

---

3. God wants us to be "sanctified" (v. 3), or "set apart," for his purposes. In what ways should our lives be clearly different from those who do not know God (vv. 3-5)?

---

4. Odysseus ordered his men to stop their ears with beeswax and to tie him to the mast. What precautions can we take to avoid sexual immorality?

---

5. Paul warns us against wronging or taking advantage of each other sexually (v. 6). When we are sexually immoral, how do we hurt others as well as ourselves?

---

6. According to verse 6 the Lord will punish those who do not follow

Paul's warning. Since Paul is writing to Christians, what do you think he means by this?

---

7. People often think of sexual restraint as puritanical or Victorian—in other words as humanly made rules that we can reject. Yet when we commit sexual sins, how do we reject God himself and the Holy Spirit (vv. 7-8)?

---

8. "Brotherly love" (v. 9) refers to the love between members of the same family. In what ways should we treat people in the church as part of our own family?

How can brotherly love also make sexual immorality be less of a problem in the church?

---

9. Why would those outside of the church have greater respect for Christians if we followed Paul's advice in verses 11-12?

---

10. Why do you think the kind of life Paul describes throughout this passage is pleasing to God?

11. In what area does this passage call you to change?

Ask God to enable you to please him more in more in each of the areas Paul mentioned in this passage.

Now or Later

In what ways should you be different from non-Christians in the programs you watch on TV, the movies you view or the books and magazines you read? What is the difference between being wise and being legalistic when it comes to these sources of sexual temptation?

7

Keeping
the Peace

Romans 14

"Mark Twain once said that he put a dog and a cat together in a cage as an experiment, to see if they could get along. They did, so he put in a bird, pig, and goat. They, too, got along fine after a few adjustments. Then he put in a Baptist, Presbyterian, and Catholic; soon there was not a living thing left."*

GROUP DISCUSSION. Jesus told his followers, "By this all men will know that you are my disciples, if you love one another" (John 13:35). But unfortunately the church has often been characterized more by fighting, divisions and disputes than by love. Why do you think this is so?

PERSONAL REFLECTION. How might a loving, peaceful community of Christians be very attractive to non-Christians in our culture?

In Romans 14 Paul tells us how to please God by peacefully resolving our conflicts. *Read Romans 14.*

---

1. Throughout this passage Paul describes people whose "faith is weak." What do you think he means by that description?

---

2. Paul refers to "disputable matters" in verse 1. What are some gray areas in which godly Christians disagree?

---

3. Why are we prone to pass judgment on those who disagree with us and to look down on them or condemn them (vv. 1-3)?

---

4. According to Paul, why shouldn't we pass judgment on other Christians in these gray areas (vv. 3-12)?

---

5. In these areas of dispute why is our attitude toward God more important than being "right" (vv. 5-9)?

---

6. In light of God's future judgment (vv. 10-12), why is it pointless for us to judge or look down on other Christians?

---

7. What does it mean to put a "stumbling block" or "obstacle" in someone's way (vv. 13-21)?

_____

8. Why do you think God is pleased (v. 18) when we give up some of our freedoms for the sake of other Christians?

Why would this sort of behavior also be approved of by others (v. 18)?

_____

9. If we believe certain practices are acceptable which others feel are sinful, then according to verse 22 why is it best to keep our beliefs between ourselves and God?

_____

10. In deciding whether we should or should not do certain things, why is it important to listen to our inner thoughts and feelings (vv. 22-23)?

_____

11. In what ways would you like the teaching in this chapter to impact your relationships and behavior?

Ask God to help you to be less judgmental and more sensitive to the needs of those whose "faith is weak."

Now or Later

Identify one area in which you are judgmental of those who either seem too legalistic of too permissive in their practices. How can Paul's words in Romans 14 help you see these people as God sees them?

8

Obeying His Commands

1 John 3:11-24

King Solomon's first great act of wisdom concerned two prostitutes and a baby. When both women insisted that the baby was theirs, Solomon commanded that the child be cut in two, so that each woman could have half.

One of the women cried out, "Please, my lord, give her the living baby! Don't kill him!" But the other woman said, "Neither I nor you shall have him. Cut him in two!" "Then the king gave this ruling: 'Give the living baby to the first woman. Do not kill him. She is his mother' " (1 Kings 3:16-28).

How did Solomon know that the first woman was the true mother? Was he merely guessing, or did he know something about the way mothers behave?

GROUP DISCUSSION. Play two truths and a lie. Each person tells two things about him or herself that are true and two that are a lie. The group tries to guess which is the lie.

PERSONAL REFLECTION. Why do you think Solomon could be confident about his "test" to reveal the child's true mother?

The apostle John describes how our behavior can reveal whether we are children of God. Read *1 John 3:11-24*.

---

1. As you read this passage, what were some of the contrasts you noticed?

---

2. How does the "message" John writes about in verse 11 express the heart of Christianity?

---

3. According to John, what do Cain, the evil one and the world have in common (vv. 12-15)?

In contrast to Cain, what do his brother Abel and the children of God have in common?

---

4. How does the presence or absence of love reveal our true spiritual condition (vv. 14-15)?

---

5. How does Christ's death on the cross (v. 16) reveal to us the meaning of love?

6. Few of us will ever have the chance to literally lay down our lives for other Christians. But how can we demonstrate a sacrificial love toward each other (vv. 17-18)?

In what ways do you see this kind of love expressed within the Christian community?

7. In addition to helping others, how can a life of love have a positive impact on our hearts (vv. 19-21)?

8. Why is it also reassuring to know that God is greater than our hearts and knows everything (v. 20)?

9. When we obey God's commands and do what pleases him, why can we be confident that he will answer our prayers (vv. 21-24)?

10. When you look at other Christians in your church and community, what needs do you see?

11. How can you lovingly meet those needs—not just with words but with actions?

Ask God to make you more sensitive to the needs of those around you. Pray that he will make you a more compassionate and loving person.

Now or Later

Identify one or two people in your church who need a ministry of love and compassion. (Think of those who are sick, in financial difficulty, lonely or in the midst of a crisis.) How can you love them sacrificially during this difficult time in their lives?

9

Keeping
Your Balance

Psalm 73

When I was in the seventh grade, a group of us went swimming in a pond at the old Skillern's farm. Our diving board was a flat cement spillway covered with wet moss that broke off just at the water's edge. As I was walking on the moss getting ready for my next dive, my feet suddenly slipped out from under me. Instinctively I reached out my arms to break my fall, but they too slipped, and my face slammed against the cement. When I lifted my head, I spit out broken fragments of my two front teeth. You should have heard my mother after I went home and gave her a big smile!

GROUP DISCUSSION. Tell about an accident, from childhood or adulthood, where you lost your balance and hurt yourself, or at least your pride.

PERSONAL REFLECTION. Think of a time when you slipped and fell spiritually. What caused you to slip?

In Psalm 73 the writer describes a time when his feet almost slipped. Although he was trying his best to serve God, he noticed that the wicked seemed to have a better, more prosperous life than he did. If you have ever wondered whether it's worth it to please God, then this psalm can help you keep your balance and your perspective. *Read Psalm 73.*

---

1. The psalmist begins by affirming God's goodness to those who are pure in heart (v. 1). Yet how did his experience begin to challenge that belief (vv. 2-3)?

---

2. Does it ever bother you when you see non-Christians who have a richer, fuller life than you do? Why?

---

3. In verses 4-12 the wicked are not viewed objectively but rather through the eyes of envy. What are some of the things about the wicked that really bother the psalmist?

---

4. Why does the condition of the wicked seem totally unfair to the psalmist, especially when he looks at his own life (vv. 13-14)?

---

5. Have you ever felt like giving up on the Christian life because it didn't seem worth the effort? Explain.

6. Why do you think the psalmist was able to regain both his balance and his perspective by entering God's sanctuary (vv. 15-17)?

7. By spending time in God's presence, what new insights did the psalmist discover about the wicked (vv. 18-20)?

8. After going into God's sanctuary, how did the psalmist's view of his own life and values undergo a radical reversal (vv. 21-26)?

9. If we want to spend our entire lives pleasing God, then in what ways would it be helpful to view everyday events from an eternal perspective?

Why must we also value our relationship with God more than anything or anyone else?

10. To what extent can you proclaim with the psalmist, "Whom have I in heaven but you? And earth has nothing I desire besides you" (v. 25)? Explain.

11. The psalmist concludes with a vow to tell others about God's deeds (v. 28)—a vow he fulfilled in part by writing and singing this psalm. In what ways can you celebrate God's goodness to you?

Pray that your love for God will become your greatest passion and your highest motivation.

Now or Later

Take time this week to meditate on the events of your life—both past and present—from an eternal perspective. Then celebrate God's goodness by either praying some of the psalms of praise or singing some of your favorite hymns.

Leader's Notes

Leading a Bible discussion can be an enjoyable and rewarding experience. But it can also be *scary*—especially if you've never done it before. If this is your feeling, you're in good company. When God asked Moses to lead the Israelites out of Egypt, he replied, "O Lord, please send someone else to do it!" (Ex 4:13). It was the same with Solomon, Jeremiah and Timothy, but God helped these people in spite of their weaknesses, and he will help you as well.

You don't need to be an expert on the Bible or a trained teacher to lead a Bible discussion. The idea behind these inductive studies is that the leader guides group members to discover for themselves what the Bible has to say. This method of learning will allow group members to remember much more of what is said than a lecture would.

These studies are designed to be led easily. As a matter of fact, the flow of questions through the passage from observation to interpretation to application is so natural that you may feel that the studies lead themselves. This study guide is also flexible. You can use it with a variety of groups— student, professional, neighborhood or church groups. Each study takes forty-five to sixty minutes in a group setting.

There are some important facts to know about group dynamics and encouraging discussion. The suggestions listed below should enable you to effectively and enjoyably fulfill your role as leader.

Preparing for the Study

1. Ask God to help you understand and apply the passage in your own life. Unless this happens, you will not be prepared to lead others. Pray too for the various members of the group. Ask God to open your hearts to the message of his Word and motivate you to action.

2. Read the introduction to the entire guide to get an overview of the entire book and the issues which will be explored.

3. As you begin each study, read and reread the assigned Bible passage to familiarize yourself with it.

4. This study guide is based on the New International Version of the Bible. It will help you and the group if you use this translation as the basis for your study and discussion.

5. Carefully work through each question in the study. Spend time in meditation and reflection as you consider how to respond.

6. Write your thoughts and responses in the space provided in the study guide. This will help you to express your understanding of the passage clearly.

7. It might help to have a Bible dictionary handy. Use it to look up any unfamiliar words, names or places. (For additional help on how to study a passage, see chapter five of *How Lead a LifeGuide Bible Study,* InterVarsity Press.)

8. Consider how you can apply the Scripture to your life. Remember that the group will follow your lead in responding to the studies. They will not go any deeper than you do.

9. Once you have finished your own study of the passage, familiarize yourself with the leader's notes for the study you are leading. These are designed to help you in several ways. First, they tell you the purpose the study guide author had in mind when writing the study. Take time to think through how the study questions work together to accomplish that purpose. Second, the notes provide you with additional background information or suggestions on group dynamics for various questions. This information can be useful when people have difficulty understanding or answering a question. Third, the leader's notes can alert you to potential problems you may encounter during the study.

10. If you wish to remind yourself of anything mentioned in the leader's notes, make a note to yourself below that question in the study.

Leading the Study

1. Begin the study on time. Open with prayer, asking God to help the group to understand and apply the passage.

2. Be sure that everyone in your group has a study guide. Encourage the

group to prepare beforehand for each discussion by reading the introduction to the guide and by working through the questions in the study.

3. At the beginning of your first time together, explain that these studies are meant to be discussions, not lectures. Encourage the members of the group to participate. However, do not put pressure on those who may be hesitant to speak during the first few sessions. You may want to suggest the following guidelines to your group.

☐ Stick to the topic being discussed.

☐ Your responses should be based on the verses which are the focus of the discussion and not on outside authorities such as commentaries or speakers.

☐ These studies focus on a particular passage of Scripture. Only rarely should you refer to other portions of the Bible. This allows for everyone to participate in in-depth study on equal ground.

☐ Anything said in the group is considered confidential and will not be discussed outside the group unless specific permission is given to do so.

☐ We will listen attentively to each other and provide time for each person present to talk.

☐ We will pray for each other.

4. Have a group member read the introduction at the beginning of the discussion.

5. Every session begins with a group discussion question. The question or activity is meant to be used before the passage is read. The question introduces the theme of the study and encourages group members to begin to open up. Encourage as many members as possible to participate and be ready to get the discussion going with your own response.

This section is designed to reveal where our thoughts or feelings need to be transformed by Scripture. That is why it is especially important not to read the passage before the discussion question is asked. The passage will tend to color the honest reactions people would otherwise give because they are, of course, supposed to think the way the Bible does.

You may want to supplement the group discussion question with an icebreaker to help people to get comfortable. See the community section of *Small Group Idea Book* for more ideas.

You also might want to use the personal reflection question with your group. Either allow a time of silence for people to respond individually or discuss it together.

6. Have a group member (or members if the passage is long) read aloud the passage to be studied. Then give people several minutes to read the passage again silently so that they can take it all in.

7. Question 1 will generally be an overview question designed to briefly survey the passage. Encourage the group to briefly survey the passage, but try to avoid getting sidetracked by questions or issues that will be addressed later in the study.

8. As you ask the questions, keep in mind that they are designed to be used just as they are written. You may simply read them aloud. Or you may prefer to express them in your own words.

There may be times when it is appropriate to deviate from the study guide. For example, a question may have already been answered. If so, move on to the next question. Or someone may raise an important question not covered in the guide. Take time to discuss it, but try to keep the group from going off on tangents.

9. Avoid answering your own questions. If necessary, repeat or rephrase them until they are clearly understood. Or point out something you read in the leader's notes to clarify the context or meaning. An eager group quickly becomes passive and silent if they think the leader will do most of the talking.

10. Don't be afraid of silence. People may need time to think about the question before formulating their answers.

11. Don't be content with just one answer. Ask, "What do the rest of you think?" or "Anything else?" until several people have given answers to the question.

12. Acknowledge all contributions. Try to be affirming whenever possible. Never reject an answer. If it is clearly off-base, ask, "Which verse led you to that conclusion?" or again, "What do the rest of you think?"

13. Don't expect every answer to be addressed to you, even though this will probably happen at first. As group members become more at ease, they will begin to truly interact with each other. This is one sign of healthy discussion.

14. Don't be afraid of controversy. It can be very stimulating. If you don't resolve an issue completely, don't be frustrated. Move on and keep it in mind for later. A subsequent study may solve the problem.

15. Periodically summarize what the group has said about the passage. This helps to draw together the various ideas mentioned and gives continuity to the study. But don't preach.

16. At the end of the Bible discussion you may want to allow group members a time of quiet to work on an idea under "Now or Later." Then discuss what you experienced. Or you may want to encourage group members to work on these ideas between meetings. Give an opportunity during the session to allow people to talk about what they are learning.

17. Conclude your time together with conversational prayer, adapting the prayer suggestion at the end of the study to your group. Ask for God's help in following through on the commitments you've made.

18. End on time.

Many more suggestions and helps are found in *How to Lead a LifeGuide Bible Study,* which is part of the LifeGuide Bible Study series.

Components of Small Groups

A healthy small group should do more than study the Bible. There are four components to consider as you structure your time together.

Nurture. Small groups help us to grow in our knowledge and love of God. Bible study is the key to making this happen and is the foundation of your small group.

Community. Small groups are a great place to develop deep friendships with other Christians. Allow time for informal interaction before and after each study. Plan activities and games that will help you to get to know each other. Spend time having fun together—going on a picnic or cooking dinner together.

Worship and prayer. Your study will be enhanced by spending time praising God together in prayer or song. Pray for each other's needs—and keep track of how God is answering prayer in your group. Ask God to help you to apply what you are learning in your study.

Outreach. Reaching out to others can be a practical way of applying what you are learning, and it will keep your group from becoming self-focused. Host a series of evangelistic discussions for your friends or neighbors. Clean up the yard of an elderly friend. Serve at a soup kitchen together, or spend a day working on a Habitat house.

Many more suggestions and helps in each of these areas are found in

Small Group Idea Book. Information on building a small group can be found in *Small Group Leaders' Handbook* and *The Big Book on Small Groups* (both from InterVarsity Press). Reading through one of these books would be worth your time.

Study 1. Perfectly Pleasing. Hebrews 10:1-25.

Purpose: To realize that Jesus has made us perfectly pleasing to God—forever.

Question 2. By making such statements as "it can never, by the same sacrifices repeated endlessly year after year, make perfect those who draw near to worship" the author of Hebrews stresses that (1) there was never an end to these sacrifices, (2) there was never an end to the number of years they were offered, and (3) there was never an end to the guilt these sacrifices were supposed to cleanse.

Question 3. Instead of cleansing the consciences of those who offered them, the sacrifices were instead an annual reminder of uncleansed guilt.

Question 4. The *NIV Bible Commentary* states, "Animal sacrifices could not take away the sins of the people. But it was the will of God that sin be atoned for. Christ's perfect sacrifice of himself fulfills God's will as animal sacrifices could never do. This the author sees foretold in Ps 40" (*NIV Bible Commentary,* vol. 2: *New Testament,* eds. Kenneth L. Barker & John Kohlenberger III [Grand Rapids: Zondervan, 1994], p. 985).

Question 5. Add a note here to expand your thought about "shadowy" practices in the original question and to explain what was offensive in these practices.

Question 6. The animal sacrifices graphically illustrated that our sins can only be cleansed by the death of a substitute. Although animals can never atone for human sins, these sacrifices pointed to the only true substitute, Jesus Christ.

Question 8. There is a very real difference between guilt, which Christ has cleansed once for all time, and guilty feelings, which may remain even though our guilt has been removed. The author of Hebrews wants us to realize that because of Christ we should no longer feel the burden of guilt.

Question 9. The notes in the *NIV Study Bible* state, "The way into the sanctuary of God's presence was closed to the people under the former covenant because the blood of animal sacrifices could never completely atone for their sins. Now, however, believers can come to the throne of grace since the perfect priest has offered the perfect sacrifice, atoning for sin once for all" (Kenneth Barker, ed. [Grand Rapids: Zondervan, 1985], p. 1870).

Study 2. Amazed by Grace. John 8:1-11.

Purpose: To discover that a life which is pleasing to God does not begin with commitment or sheer determination, but with grace.

Question 2. The *NIV Bible Commentary* explains:

> The dilemma that the scribes and Pharisees posed was this: According to the law, she should be put to death (see Lev 20:10; Dt 22:22-24). If, then, Jesus refused to confirm the death penalty, he could be charged with contradicting the law of God and would himself be liable to condemnation. If, on the other hand, he confirmed the verdict of the Pharisees, he would lose his reputation for compassion; and possibly he could have been reported to the Romans as inciting the Sanhedrin to independent exercise of the death penalty. (*NIV Bible Commentary,* vol. 2: *New Testament,* p. 322.)

Question 3. The woman's accusers obviously did not care about the woman herself, since they set a trap for her and then exposed her to public humiliation. They also did not care about true justice, since they evidently allowed the man caught in adultery to escape—possibly because he helped them set up the trap.

Question 4. For centuries scholars and Bible students have speculated about what Jesus wrote on the ground. Did he write the names of the woman's accusers? Their own private sins? The ten commandments? We can never know the answer to this question and can only speculate. Even the reason for Jesus' writing on the ground remains a mystery. Perhaps he merely wanted to give himself and the accusers time to think about the situation.

Questions 5-6. In Romans 2:1 Paul writes, "You, therefore, have no excuse, you who pass judgment on someone else, for at whatever point you judge the other, you are condemning yourself, because you who pass judgment do the same things." Jesus knows that the woman's accusers, who are so eager to see her punished for her sins, have committed many sins of their own that also deserved to be punished. His comments expose their guilty consciences.

Question 7. "The accusers 'began to go away one at a time, the older ones first.' The older ones either had more sins for which they were answerable or else had more sense than to make an impossible profession of righteousness" (*NIV Bible Commentary,* vol. 2: *New Testament,* p. 322).

Question 9. Although we may never have committed adultery, we are just as guilty as the woman and her accusers. Yet instead of condemning us for our sin, Jesus offers us grace and forgiveness—but with the strong warning, "Go now and leave your life of sin" (Jn 8:11).

Study 3. Offering Yourself to God. Romans 12:1-8.

Purpose: To understand our proper and pleasing response to God's grace.

Question 2. "Paul's summons to transform our lives does not come in a vacuum. It is only *in view of God's mercy* that his appeal becomes relevant and that our obedience of it is possible. As we recognize all (the word 'mercy' is plural in the Greek) that God has done for us in his Son, as Paul has surveyed it in chs. 1-11, we realize that offering ourselves to God *as living sacrifices* is, indeed, a 'reasonable' *(logiken)* act of worship" (*New Bible Commentary: 21st Century Edition,* eds. G. J. Wenham, J. A. Motyer, D. A. Carson and R. T. France [Downers Grove, Ill.: InterVarsity Press, 1994], p. 1150).

Questions 3-4. In contrast to the dead sacrifices of the Old Testament era, Paul urges us to present our bodies as "living sacrifices" (v. 1). Just as the various members of our bodies were formerly used to practice sin, so we should now dedicate them to the service of God. John Stott writes, "Our feet will walk in his paths, our lips will speak the truth and spread the gospel, our tongues will bring healing, our hands will lift up those who have fallen, and perform many mundane tasks as well like cooking an cleaning, typing an mending; our arms will embrace the lonely and the unloved, our ears will listen to the cries of the distressed, and our eyes will look humbly and patiently towards God" (*Romans: God's Good News for the World* [Downers Grove, Ill.: InterVarsity Press, 1994], p. 322). However, we must not think that one supreme act of dedication to God will be sufficient. Instead we must renew our sacrificial commitment to God daily.

Question 6. Spiritual transformation involves both a human and a divine participation. On the one hand, it is nothing less than a miracle: God's Spirit takes us through a metamorphosis that ultimately changes us from spiritual caterpillars, who are corrupted and damaged by sin, to spiritual butter-flies—people whose lives are as pure and lovely as Jesus Christ himself. But on the other hand, this transformation does not occur without our cooperation. As we read and meditate on God's Word and apply it to our lives, our minds become renewed with a biblical perspective. We begin to adopt God's values, priorities and commitments, and these begin to reorient the entire direction of our lives.

Question 8. "Paul urges us not to think too highly of ourselves, but to look at ourselves honestly and objectively. We are to measure ourselves, not by each other, but by *the measure of faith (metron pisteos)*. Some take this phrase to designate the differing amounts of faith that God has given each of us (cf. the NIV and RSV). The context, however, suggests that Paul is speaking here of our common Christian faith, against which each of us is to measure himself or herself (JB: 'the standard of faith'). When we do this, comparison of ourselves with other believers becomes relatively unimportant—particularly since God has given different gifts to the members of his church" (*New Bible Commentary*, pp. 1150-51.)

Question 9. The analogy of the human body helps us to realize that the biblical model is neither independence nor dependence but rather interdependence. Just as the various members of our physical bodies are interdependent, working together to make our lives possible and productive, so we too, as members of Christ's body, must work together for our growth and his glory.

Study 4. Living by Faith. Hebrews 11:1-16.

Purpose: To meet some of the members of the biblical Hall of Fame and discover why their faith was so pleasing to God.

General note. Look up the other verse references in this study and be prepared to summarize the information there rather than looking up all the verses during the study.

Question 2. "Here we discover the essential characteristics of faith from the writer's point of view. Faith deals with things future (*what we hope for*) and things unseen (*what we do not see*). The NIV translation (*being sure of what we hope for*) puts the emphasis on faith as an expression of our confidence in God's promises. However, it is also possible to translate, 'faith is the substance [*hypostasis*] of things hoped for' [AV], or 'faith gives substance to our hopes' (NEB). Such a rendering suggests that *what we hope for* becomes real and substantial by the exercise of faith. This does not mean that the gospel is true simply because we believe in it! Rather, the reality of what we hope for is confirmed for us in our experience when we live by faith in God's promises. Again, faith is being *certain of what we do not see.* It is the means of 'proving' or 'testing' invisible realities such as the existence of God, his faithfulness to his word and his control over our world and its affairs. If this definition seems abstract, its meaning becomes more concrete in the illustrations that follow" (*New Bible Commentary*, p. 1346).

Question 4. It is sometimes suggested that Abel's offering was "better" than Cain's because it was an animal sacrifice rather than the fruits of the soil. But the author of Hebrews does not focus on the nature of the sacrifice but rather on the heart of the ones offering the sacrifice. Evidently Abel offered his sacrifice by faith, and Cain did not. In other words, Abel's heart was right with God, while Cain merely went through the motions. In the Genesis account God tells Cain, "If you do what is right, will you not be accepted? But if you do not do what is right, sin is crouching at your door" (Gen 4:6-7).

Question 5. The Genesis account does say that "Enoch walked with God" (Gen 5:22, 24). Evidently to the author of Hebrews the idea of walking with God is synonymous with pleasing God. And since it is impossible to please God apart from faith, then Enoch, of necessity, must have lived by faith.

Question 6. In order to please God we must (1) "believe that he exists," and (2) that he "rewards those who earnestly seek him." Obviously, belief in God's existence is foundational, since we would never entrust our lives to someone who was merely a pious fantasy. Yet belief in God's existence— by itself—is insufficient, since even the demons believe and tremble (Jas 2:19). We must also believe that God will reward us if we diligently seek him. In other words, we must not only believe that God exists but also that he is good.

If the group doesn't pick up on the significance of believing that God exists, you might ask, "What specifically must we believe about God, and why?"

Question 8. See also Matthew 24:36-41. Some of the parallels you should look for are these: (1) Both in Noah's time and our own, God's judgment was imminent, even though "not yet seen"; (2) both then and now most people are completely unaware of the coming judgment—a situation that Jesus urges us to correct by preaching the gospel; (3) both then and now we have the responsibility of taking refuge in God's means of salvation (the ark for Noah and his family; the Savior today).

Question 10. The author of Hebrews is not saying that God never fulfills his promises in this life, since obviously he does—at least in part. Each of the heroes of faith mentioned in this chapter knew God's faithfulness firsthand. But God's promises are so great and encompassing that they can only be ultimately fulfilled when Jesus Christ returns, death is destroyed, our salvation is complete, and the heavens and earth are recreated. Like the people mentioned in this chapter, we must keep this long-term perspective if we are to endure the hardships and disappointments of life.

Study 5. Looking at Your Heart. 1 Samuel 16:1-13.

Purpose: To realize that the Lord is not pleased by external factors, such as height or appearance but rather looks at our hearts.

Question 3. Not only was Eliab tall and handsome, he was also Jesse's firstborn son (1 Sam 17:13), the one who normally would have been chosen first in Israel's culture.

Question 5. Encourage the group to explore not only outward appearance—height, beauty, clothes and so on—but also other external qualities such as position, education or influence.

To add some interest to your discussion you might want to read the following after everyone has had a chance to respond: "A University of Pittsburgh study of the last decade showed that a tall MBA graduate averages $600 more per year for each extra inch in height. In his 1994 book *The Truth About Your Height* (San Diego: Reventropy Associates), author Thomas T. Samaras agrees there are more talls in high-level jobs. He says his studies conclude that jobs traditionally biased towards tall people include corporate executives, managers, stockbrokers, television newscasters, consultants and models" (Joyce Lain Kennedy, "Want a Better Job? Grow," *Grand Rapids Press* [January 10, 1995]).

Question 7. You might ask the group to think of people they know or have known whose inner qualities and abilities far exceeded what their meek exterior might suggest.

Question 9. It is interesting that the Lord didn't simply tell Samuel that David was the one he should anoint. Instead, he allowed Samuel to go through the entire family before coming to David. Initially, Samuel used worldly criteria in supposing that Eliab was the Lord's anointed. Yet as he went down the line of Jesse's sons, the truth of verse 7 began to sink in. The process was an educational experience for Samuel and everyone else in David's family.

Study 6. Pursuing Moral Purity. 1 Thessalonians 4:1-12.

Purpose: To realize that in order to please God we must be morally pure.

Question 1. Our growth in godliness is always progressive and never complete until Jesus returns. As a result we must continue to become more and more like him in every area of our lives.

Question 3. *The Bible Knowledge Commentary: New Testament* states that

> The first instruction designed to produce greater holiness is abstinence from *sexual immorality.* Paul called his readers to *avoid* it, implying the need for exercising self-discipline, enabled by God's Spirit. Christians are to avoid and abstain from any and every form of sexual practice that lies outside the circle of God's revealed will, namely adultery, premarital and extramarital intercourse, homosexuality, and other perversions. The word *porneia,* translated "sexual immorality," is a broad one and includes all these practices. The Thessalonians lived in a pagan environment in which sexual looseness was not only practiced openly but was also encouraged. In Greek religion, prostitution was considered a priestly prerogative, and extramarital sex was sometimes an act of worship. To a Christian the will of God is clear: holiness and sexual immorality are mutually exclusive (QuickVerse 4.0 Deluxe Bible Reference Collection, Parson's Technology.)

Question 4. If your group includes both men and women, they might find it easier to be more honest with this question if you temporarily break in to two groups in which men share with men and women with women. This could also provide some variety for your discussion. But come back together for the next question.

Question 6. Although Paul could be referring to judgment during this life (see 1 Cor 11:29-30), he probably has in mind future judgment, when we will stand before Jesus Christ and "each of us will give an account of himself to God" (Rom 14:12). Paul describes this judgment in 1 Corinthians 3:10-15: "Each one should be careful how he builds. For no one can lay any foundation other than the one already laid, which is Jesus Christ. If any man builds on this foundation using gold, silver, costly stones, wood, hay or straw, his work will be shown for what it is, because the Day will bring it to light. It will be revealed with fire, and the fire will test the quality of each man's work. If what he has built survives, he will receive his reward. If it is burned up, he will suffer loss; he himself will be saved, but only as one escaping through the flames."

Question 8. Christians frequently speak of "agape love," the kind of love described in 1 Corinthians 13, but in 1 Thessalonians 4:9 Paul mentions another kind of love. Robert L. Thomas helps us to understand this love when he states, " 'Brotherly love' *(philadelphia),* an expression for attachment to one's blood relatives in secular speech, was taken over by Christianity because of the close ties within the spiritual family of God" (*The Expositor's Bible Commentary,* vol. 12, ed. Grank E. Gaebelein [Grand Rapids, Zondervan, 1981]).

Question 9. In order to answer this question it helps to understand the context of Paul's words. I. Howard Marshall writes, "Some of the people in the church were taking advantage of this brotherly love to live off charity without doing any work themselves (cf. 2 Thes. 3:6-15). These idlers may have been influenced by their belief that the second coming of Jesus was near; if so, they reasoned, why bother working? Paul instructs them to make it a matter of honour to avoid being busybodies, to look after their own affairs in a responsible way, and to be prepared to do an honest day's work. This would prevent them losing the respect of other people" (*The New Bible Commentary,* p. 1282).

Study 7. Keeping the Peace Conflicts. Romans 14.

Purpose: To discover how to please God by peacefully resolving our conflicts.

Question 2. Some examples would include drinking alcoholic beverages, working on Sunday, going to certain types of movies, listening to certain kinds of music and so on. To qualify for a "disputable matter" a practice must not be either expressly forbidden or commanded in Scripture.

Question 3. Those who believe certain practices are forbidden by God will often condemn those who engage in these practices and view such people as sinful. Likewise, those who believe such practices are permissible will often view their opponents as ignorant, repressed or unliberated. According to Paul, God is not pleased with either attitude.

Question 4. Paul gives several reasons for not passing judgment on other Christians: (1) God has accepted them, (2) they are God's servants and he will enable them to stand, (3) they are practicing what they believe to be right, and (4) God will be their final Judge.

Question 5. John Stott writes, "Whether one is an eater or an abstainer, the same two principles apply. If we are able to receive something from God with thanksgiving, as his gift to us, then we can offer it back to him. The two movements, from him to us and from us to him, belong together and are vital aspects of our Christian discipleship. Both are valuable and practical tests. 'Can I thank God for this? Can I do this unto the Lord?'" (*Romans: God's Good News for the World* [Downers Grove, Ill.: InterVarsity Press, 1994], p. 362).

Question 7. Putting a "stumbling block" or "obstacle" in someone's way means more than simply doing something they think is wrong, otherwise we would always be at the mercy of other people's opinions. Paul has in mind something far more serious. We should not do anything that might "destroy" other Christians or "cause [them] to fall" by following our example when it violates their consciences (see also 1 Cor 8:9-13). Paul isn't thinking of eternal destruction but rather of damaging their walk with God and growth in Christ.

Question 8. As Paul states in verse 17, the kingdom of God is not a matter of what we eat or drink or what morally neutral areas we do or do not practice. Rather God is primarily concerned about true righteousness, peace and joy in the Holy Spirit. If we are to avoid judging or looking down on other Christians, we must develop God's sense of values and priorities.

Question 10. Whenever the Scriptures are unclear about a matter, or whenever we are unclear about what Scripture teaches, Paul tells us that we should follow the guidance of our consciences (see also Rom 2:14-15). Evidently our consciences become the standard of right and wrong in the absence of clear biblical teaching.

Study 8. Obeying His Commands. 1 John 3:11-24.

Purpose: To understand why our behavior can reveal whether we are children of God or children of the devil.

Question 2. You may also want to look at John 13:34-35.

Question 3. In order to understand this passage it is helpful to view it in the light of its broader context. Earlier in this chapter, and in previous chapters, John had argued that everyone is either a child of God or a child of the devil. Those who are children of God resemble their heavenly Father in their beliefs, their behavior and their attitude toward others. Likewise, those who are children of the devil resemble their father in these same areas. As a result we can often tell a person's spiritual parent by the way the person acts.

Question 4. John isn't saying that everyone who loves is a Christian. Earlier in this letter he has also emphasized the importance of beliefs (2:20-23) and behavior (3:4-10). Also John's focus is not on love in general but rather on love for other members of the family of God. Love for other Christians is one of the primary evidences that we are God's children.

Question 5. You may also want to look at John 15:12-13.

Question 6. Sacrificial love is seldom a one-time act. It usually involves the ongoing practice of seeing the needs of others and doing whatever we can to meet those needs. Glen W. Barker writes, "Again John's penchant for providing practical 'tests' of the validity of one's faith comes to the fore. How can we know whether we would sacrifice our life for a brother? We can know by being compassionate toward him in his present need. If we are unable or unwilling to sacrifice material advantage for the sake of our brother, we know the love of God is not in us. What are the conditions for our involvement with our brother? If we are in a position to see *(theoreo)* with our own eyes his need, as, for example, the good Samaritan did, and can offer help, then we cannot do otherwise than act. To withhold help from a brother in need, to shut off compassionate action, is to deny the presence of God's love in one's own heart" (*NIV Bible Commentary,* vol. 2: *New Testament,* p. 1097).

Questions 7-8. Since sacrificially loving other Christians is one of the primary evidences that we are God's children, then by practicing such love we can reassure our hearts that we are truly Christians. Of course, we are both finite and fallible and therefore should leave the final judgment to

God, who is greater than our hearts and knows everything. The broader context of John's letter would indicate that if we (1) believe in Jesus Christ, (2) seek to follow God's commands and (3) love other Christians, then we should have every assurance that we are truly God's children. Love and obedience do not make us Christians, however; they are merely the evidence that we belong to God's family.

Question 9. Leon Morris writes, "Receiving answers to prayer does not at first sight follow on from the fact that our heart does not condemn us. But confidence is common to both, and answered prayer inevitably increases our confidence. Both *obey* and *do* are in continuous tenses. Power in prayer does not come from occasional bursts of obedience, but from lives of habitual obedience. Further, believers do *what pleases him.* This goes beyond the keeping of the commandments. Just as in the Sermon on the Mount there is a concern for the spirit of the commandments; it is not enough to keep the letter of the law" (*New Bible Commentary,* p. 1405).

Question 11. Encourage the group to think not only of how they might individually meet those needs but also as a small group and as a church.

Study 9. Keeping Your Balance. Psalm 73.

Purpose: To explore why it is worth it to please God even when life doesn't seem fair.

Question 1. The psalmist wonders whether he has wasted his time living a righteous life, especially since he seems to suffer while the wicked prosper. In other words, he questions whether it's worth it to follow God.

Question 2. Obviously, there will always be people who are richer, smarter, more successful and even happier than we are. Yet this question is designed to go beyond this. How can it be possible for those who do not know God to have a richer fuller life than those who have been given "abundant life" through Jesus Christ?

Question 3. The psalmist mentions a number of things about the wicked that really bother him: (1) "they have no struggles," (2) "their bodies are healthy and strong," (3) "they are free from the burdens common to man," (4) they are proud, (5) they are violent, (6) they are callous, conceited and full of evil and iniquity, (7) they are malicious and arrogant, (8) they seem to be able to do all this without God's judgment.

Questions 6-7. Bruce K. Waltke writes, "Overwhelmed by the greatness, glory, and majesty of God, the psalmist regained a proper perspective of his situation. He rediscovered something he had known but had forgotten: the Lord is just! In the end evil is not and never will be victorious. The wicked will be severely judged" (*The Expositor's Bible Commentary,* vol. 5, ed. Frank E. Gaebelein [Grand Rapids, Zondervan, 1981]).

Question 8. The psalmist rediscovers that he has the greatest gift of all: a relationship with God. The Lord is always with him, guiding and directing his life, and eventually the Lord will receive the psalmist into eternal glory.

Question 11. The prayers of the psalms are written with "anticipation of the expected answer to prayer." "They reflect Israel's religious conscious-ness that praise must follow deliverance as surely as prayer springs from need—if God is to be truly honored. Such praise was usually offered with thank offerings and involved celebrating God's saving act in the presence of those assembled at the temple" (*NIV Study Bible,* p. 793).

Jack Kuhatschek is Senior Acquisitions Editor at Zondervan Publishing. He is also the author of Applying the Bible *and five LifeGuide® Bible Studies.*

What Should We Study Next?

A good place to start your study of Scripture would be with a book study. Many groups begin with a Gospel such as *Mark* (22 studies by Jim Hoover) or *John* (26 studies by Douglas Connelly). These guides are divided into two parts so that if twenty-two or twenty-six weeks seems like too much to do at once, the group can feel free to do half and take a break with another topic. Later you might want to come back to it. You might prefer to try a shorter letter. *Philippians* (9 studies by Donald Baker), *Ephesians* (13 studies by Andrew T. and Phyllis J. Le Peau) and *1 & 2 Timothy and Titus* (12 studies by Pete Sommer) are good options. If you want to vary your reading with an Old Testament book, consider *Ecclesiastes* (12 studies by Bill and Teresa Syrios) for a challenging and exciting study.

There are a number of interesting topical LifeGuide studies as well. Here are some options for filling three or four quarters of a year:

Basic Discipleship
Christian Beliefs, 12 studies by Stephen D. Eyre
Christian Character, 12 studies by Andrea Sterk & Peter Scazzero
Christian Disciplines, 12 studies by Andrea Sterk & Peter Scazzero
Evangelism, 12 studies by Rebecca Pippert & Ruth Siemens

Building Community
Christian Community, 12 studies by Rob Suggs
Fruit of the Spirit, 9 studies by Hazel Offner
Spiritual Gifts, 12 studies by Charles & Anne Hummel

Character Studies
New Testament Characters, 12 studies by Carolyn Nystrom
Old Testament Characters, 12 studies by Peter Scazzero
Old Testament Kings, 12 studies by Carolyn Nystrom
Women of the Old Testament, 12 studies by Gladys Hunt

The Trinity
Meeting God, 12 studies by J. I. Packer
Meeting Jesus, 13 studies by Leighton Ford
Meeting the Spirit, 12 studies by Douglas Connelly

Other LifeGuide® Bible Studies by Jack Kuhatschek

David (12 studies)
Self-Esteem (9 studies)
Spiritual Warfare (9 studies, available July 1999)
Suffering (10 studies)
Romans (21 studies)
Galatians (12 studies)

ALSO FOR SMALL GROUPS

As well as over 70 titles in the popular *LifeBuilder* series, Scripture Union produces a wide variety of resources for small groups. Among them are:

WordLive – an innovative online Bible experience for groups and individuals, offering a wide variety of free material: study notes, maps, illustrations, images, poems, meditations, downloadable podcasts, prayer activities. Log on and check it out: www.wordlive.org

The Multi-Sensory series – popular resources for creative small groups, youth groups and churches that appeal to a wide range of learning styles.

Deeper Encounter – for confident groups that have a good understanding of Bible text – containing seven studies, complete with CD audio tracks and photocopiable worksheets.

Top Tips on Leading Small Groups – biblical patterns and practical ideas to inspire leaders of small groups.

Essential 100 and *Essential Jesus* – 100-reading overview of the Bible (*Essential 100*) and the person and work of Jesus (*Essential Jesus*), with notes and helps – presented as a programme for individuals, small groups or whole churches.

Small Groups Growing Churches – a flexible training resource for leading small groups. Can be used as a complete 15-topic training course, for a tailor-made church weekend or for one-off refresher sessions.

SU publications are available from Christian bookshops, on the Internet, or via mail order. Advice on what would suit your group best is always available. You can:

- log on to www.scriptureunion.org.uk
- phone SU's mail order line: 01908 856006
- email info@scriptureunion.org.uk
- fax 01908 856020
- write to SU Mail Order, PO Box 5148, Milton Keynes MLO, MK2 2YX

Scripture Union
Using the Bible to inspire children, young people and adults to know God.

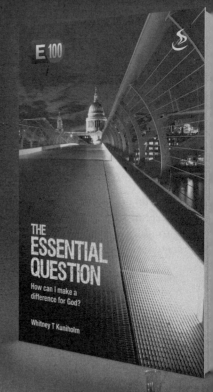